Intergalactic Travel, Cloud riders and other stories

Steve Barlow and Steve Skidmore
Mark Robertson, Robin Boyden, Mark Long
and Juan Oliver

Contents

Castle in the Air	3
What's the Time Mr Wolf?	27
A Trip to the Zoo	40
Aliens!	62

CASTLE IN THE AIR

Written by Steve Barlow
and Steve Skidmore
Illustrated by
Mark Robertson

New Laputa, Venus, 2121 CE

"Mikey?"

Without waiting for his brother's reply, Gus continued with his essay.

Earth has been sending space probes to Venus for more than a hundred and fifty years. These probes have studied the planet's atmosphere and every square metre of its surface. In the last twenty years, four cloud cities – our own New Laputa, Cloud Nine, Novograd and Vorolat – have been set up. In all that time, no intelligent life has ever been found on Venus.

"Mikey!"

Gus sighed, exasperated. Where was the kid? He shook his head and looked back at the screen. Nearly there.

He continued …

The surface of Venus is hot enough to melt lead and no living thing can exist there. The only life forms that have ever been found on Venus are mindless creatures, gasbags, and their predators, skysquid, floating in the clouds. All evidence suggests that there is no intelligent life as we know it on Venus.

Done! Gus addressed his essay – *Can Intelligent Life Exist on Venus? Explain Your Answer* – to his tutor and jabbed the SEND key. He settled his lanky frame back in his chair with a sigh of relief. He'd managed to get his homework finished – no thanks to Mikey, who had been bugging him all morning.

The incoming call signal flashed on his computer screen and within seconds, his mother's face appeared. "Hi, Gus. Everything OK there?"

"Sure," replied Gus. It didn't seem a good moment to admit that he didn't know where his little brother was – especially as he had spent all yesterday evening convincing his parents that he could look after him while they visited friends on Cloud Nine. "Mum," he remembered saying, "this is Venus! What is there to worry about? Nothing ever happens here …"

"We're just waiting for the shuttle so we'll be back in about four hours."

"See you then." Gus broke the connection and turned off his computer. He checked his watch. 18:00 hours – dinner time! Gus frowned. Mikey *never* missed meals. The first shivers of alarm slid down the back of Gus's neck.

Gus began to search the apartment. He checked every room. No Mikey.

Gus thought back to the morning. He'd been trying to get his essay done and Mikey had been all over him like a rash – "Will you play Space Marines with me? What are you doing? Will you take me cloud riding?" Eventually, Gus had lost his temper and snapped at Mikey. What had he said? Oh, yes – "Why don't you go lose yourself?"

Gus's mouth felt dry. Maybe Mikey had done exactly that.

Yet how could anyone manage to lose themselves in a cloud city floating fifty kilometres above the surface of Venus?

Gus thought hard. Where could his brother have gone?

A friend's apartment – it was obvious. Mikey had just gone to annoy somebody else. No need to panic. He just had to go and find him.

An hour later, Gus *was* starting to panic. He had tried the apartments of every one of Mikey's friends – it was hard to believe that his irritating little brother had so many. Nobody had seen Mikey.

The mall. Maybe he was there hanging out with friends. Yes, that'll be it.

He hurriedly skirted around the mall, peering into all the shops and cafés. No sign of Mikey. Gus had already tried the tiny park, with its smooth lawn and chattering songbirds from back home on Earth. Still no sign. He'd called in at the shuttle port too, thinking maybe Mikey had gone there early to meet his parents. Again, no sign. Mikey seemed to have vanished into thin air and on a cloud city of only six thousand people, Gus was running out of places to look.

He was going to be in so much trouble. He'd promised his parents he'd look after Mikey and he hadn't even noticed him going out!

The longer Gus looked for Mikey, the more frenzied his search became. An hour ago, the cloud city had seemed boringly safe. Now … Gus shivered as he started to consider all the things that could go wrong for settlers on an alien world.

Maybe a section of the city had sprung a leak. The walls of the geodesic dome that protected New Laputa, though strong, were very thin – they needed to be on a floating city. Maybe the poisonous carbon-dioxide atmosphere of Venus was seeping in and Mikey was trapped somewhere and struggling to breathe …

Gus shook himself angrily. That couldn't happen. There had been no leak alarm and even if there was a leak, this high up in the clouds the atmospheric pressure of Venus was near Earth normal. It would take hours for the Earth atmosphere to leak out and Venusian air to leak in.

No sooner had Gus dismissed that thought than it was replaced by another, even more frightening one. What if – Gus felt as though he'd swallowed an ice cube – what if Mikey had left the city?

It was a possibility that didn't bear thinking about. As Mikey fell towards the surface of Venus, he would be crushed by the terrible pressure of the dense atmosphere. If that didn't finish him off, he would be baked alive in the searing temperatures of the lower air long before he hit the planet's surface.

Again, Gus told himself to get a grip. How could Mikey possibly fall? From where? It wasn't as if New Laputa had any open windows, or balconies. The geodesic dome encased the whole city. There was only the shuttle port, and the much smaller launch ramp from which the fliers took off … Gus stopped dead in his tracks. His heart stopped. Mikey had asked Gus to take him cloud riding, and Gus had ignored him. Could Mikey have gone flying by himself?

Gus arrived at the launch ramp at a flat-out run. He spotted the duty attendant and his heart sank. The man was a know-nothing, new arrival from Earth. He looked like he still had grass stains on his knees.

Gus grabbed the man's arm. "Have you seen my little brother? Eight years old, short hair, dark like mine, freckles?"

The man scratched his head. "Kinda skinny-looking?"

Gus nodded.

"Sure, I remember him. He wanted to go flying. I rented him an acid suit, a breather and some wings."

Gus groaned. "He's too *young* to go out riding on his own! He's only done a couple of training flights! It took me three years to get my solo wings. Why did you let him go?"

The man looked worried. "Gee, I didn't realize – I'm new here …"

Gus wanted to yell Venusian curses at the groundsider ("Worm! Soil kisser!"). However, he knew that, though this might make him feel better, it wouldn't help Mikey.

"Listen," he told the man. "Call Search and Rescue. Tell them what's happened."

"Sure." The man reached for his communicator as Gus opened his locker to take out his own flying gear. "Hey, where are you going?" the attendant cried to Gus.

Gus stared at him. "I'm going after my brother, where do you think I'm going?"

"But the weather boys just called," the man whined. "There's a storm coming. I'm not supposed to let anyone else go out."

"You let Mikey go out," Gus reminded him grimly as he struggled into his acid suit, "so you're going to let me go out – and you'll loan me a spare breather. If Mikey's lost, he must be running short of air by now."

The by-now-worried attendant was still explaining the situation to Search and Rescue when Gus finished strapping on his wings, checked the air supply from his breather, and launched himself into the twisting, tumbling clouds of Venus.

Gus drew in his breath sharply. The storm was already upon him. A shower of acid rain hit him and the wind clutched at his wings with spiteful fingers. The visibility was poor – but then, in the clouds of Venus, it usually was. The tiny navigation computer in his facemask displayed all the flight data he needed. He felt comforted by the pulsing yellow signal of the New Laputa beacon that would guide him home – and Mikey, too, if Gus could find him. The way things were right now, that wasn't going to be easy. The storm would make flying difficult and the locator beacon on Mikey's flying gear, with its limited range, would be even harder to spot.

Gus felt a chill grip his body. Up until now, he'd just been annoyed with Mikey for making his life difficult. Now the harsh reality hit him – his brother was missing in this storm. Gus forgot his anger. He felt only concern for his brother.

The wind continued to tug at his wings as Gus swooped around a clump of migrating gasbags whose bloated bodies and long trailing tendrils were a common sight among the Venusian clouds. The huge, mindless creatures looked like aerial versions of the jellyfish that lived in Earth's oceans. Close behind them, a pack of skysquid were circling, moving ever closer. The long, tubular body of a skysquid darted toward the gasbags, its clutching tentacles with beak-like tips tearing at the flesh of its prey. One of the skyquid's long tentacles snapped irritably at Gus as it passed but he ignored it. Skysquid weren't nearly tough enough to tangle with their new neighbours from Earth and both they and the cloud riders knew it.

Ever since Gus had passed his final flight test and been allowed to fly solo, he had gloried in the freedom he'd found riding the clouds of Venus. He'd been born on New Laputa, one of the first generation of settlers not to start life on Earth. Gus had never seen an ocean, a desert, a forest or a mountain. The city dome could feel claustrophobic at times but out here the closed-in feeling disappeared. Real flying was something groundsiders couldn't do. Earth's gravity made them just too heavy for wings to work – but on Venus, with its lower gravity, Gus could swoop and soar among the clouds. Could his earthbound ancestors have even dreamt of such a freedom?

Yet today, everything was different. He wasn't out here to enjoy himself – he had a mission. Acid rain streamed down his mask, blurring his vision. Thunder echoed around him and lighting flickered among the writhing clouds. Gus started to feel sick as his wings were battered and twisted by savage currents of air.

Struggling to keep control, he tried not to imagine how scared Mikey must be. His brother had only ever flown in calm air under strict supervision. For the first time, Gus wondered whether he would ever find Mikey alive. His heart thudded painfully as he scanned his instruments for a sign of Mikey's locator beacon. Nothing.

Suddenly, Gus was aware of shapes in the clouds on either side of him – winged, bird-like creatures totally unlike the lumbering gasbags or torpedo-like squid. He jerked his head from side to side, trying to get a clear glimpse of them but they remained just out of his field of vision. He could only see their blurred forms moving through the misty walls of the clouds. They were close but out of reach.

The creatures were fast. They flew gracefully around Gus, apparently unconcerned by the storm. Gus's own movements were clumsy and uncontrolled in comparison. He checked his suit's radar. Nothing. Fellow cloud riders would have shown up as echoes on the display. Whatever these beings were, they left no trace on his instruments.

Gradually, Gus became aware of something else. The elusive creatures seemed to be steering him in a particular direction. He tested this by turning to one side. Instantly, the creatures came together, blocking his path. Obediently, Gus resumed his former course.

What *were* these creatures? He'd never seen or even heard of anything like them. Were they predators like the skysquid? In that case, were they herding him towards some terrible, unknown fate?

Somehow, their behaviour didn't feel threatening like that, though. Gus had a feeling it wasn't just purposeful but intelligent. It sounded crazy but it didn't seem as if they were driving him – they seemed to be *guiding* him.

As he flew further, the thunder receded, the lightning died and the rain eased. Then without warning, Gus found himself flying in clear air. He stared at the sight that met him and would have rubbed his eyes if his facemask hadn't been in the way.

Floating in front of him was a raft of gasbags, tied together like balloons by their trailing tentacles. And in the centre of the raft was …

"Mikey!"

Gus had no thought but to reach his brother as soon as possible. He dived towards the raft, pulling up at the last second with a jerk that almost tore his weather-beaten wings from his shoulders. He landed beside his brother on the soft, spongy gasbags. "Mikey, are you OK?"

"Gus …" Mikey gestured towards his breather. Hurriedly, Gus attached the spare he had brought to his brother's facemask.

Mikey took a couple of deep, thankful breaths. Then he looked up into his brother's eyes with an expression of wonder. "Gus, they saved me!"

Gus was so relieved at finding Mikey alive that he had almost forgotten the shapes in the clouds. "Who saved you, Mikey?"

"I … I don't know." Mikey shook his head. "I never saw them properly but they found me and brought me here. They were kind; they looked after me."

"Mikey, that's impossible. There aren't any intelligent beings here on Venus, you know that."

However, there was no conviction in his words. He didn't believe what he was saying either.

Mikey was right. Something – or someone – had tied the gasbags together to make a safe haven for Mikey until help arrived. Something – or someone – had also led Gus here just in the nick of time.

Mikey said stubbornly, "They *knew* what they were doing."

Gus made sure his brother was comfortable. Then he looked up at the surrounding clouds. His mind was whirring.

If Mikey was right, then the creatures that found him had shown intelligence and compassion. Yet humans had lived in the Venusian atmosphere for thirty years. They had studied the planet and declared that there were no higher life forms on Venus. That was a scientific fact. Then Gus remembered that the creatures he'd seen in the clouds hadn't registered on his suit's instruments …

Had they been there all the time but no one had ever seen them?

Or had both he and Mikey been imagining things. There couldn't really be intelligent beings living among the Venusian clouds …
… could there?

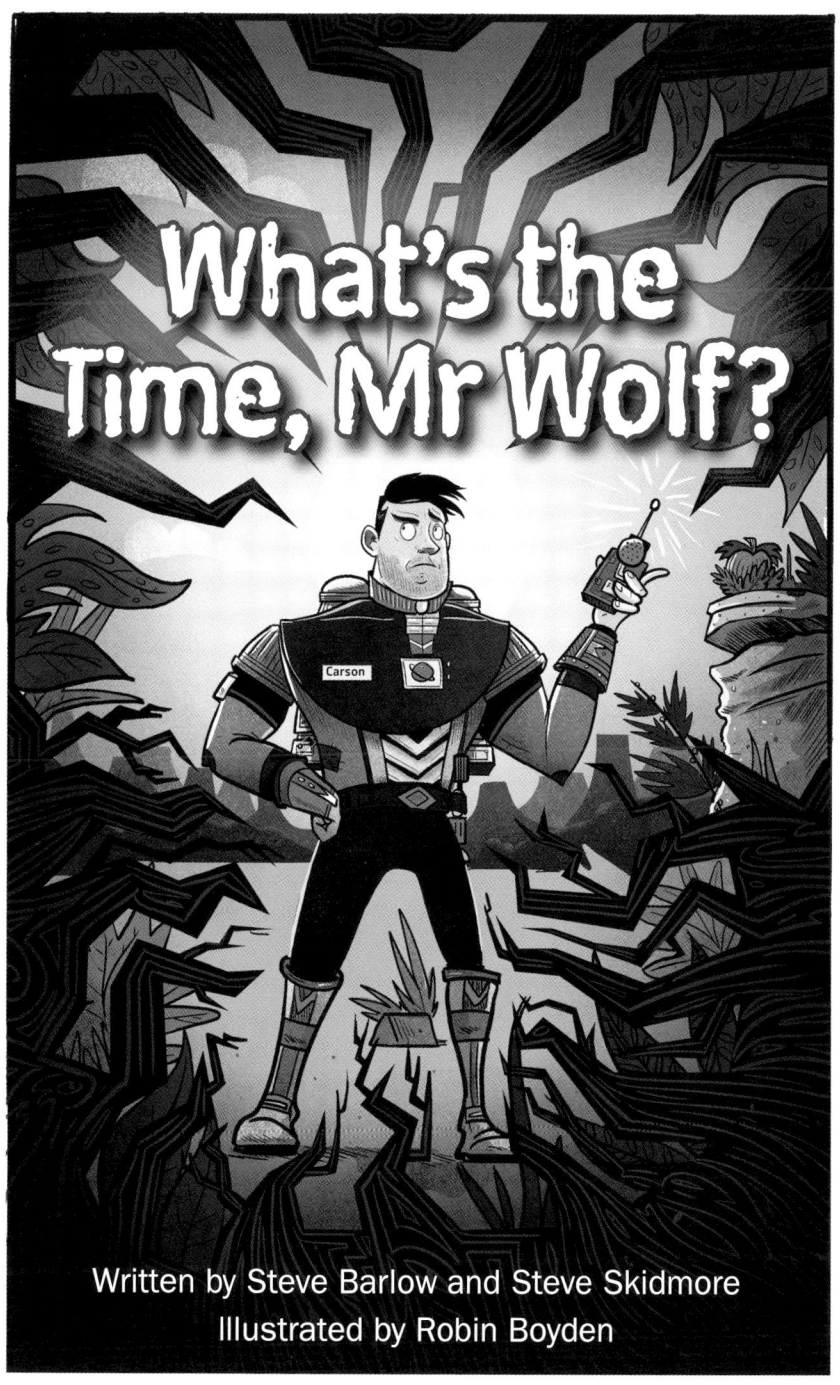

Relax. These planets are always dull. There's never anything dangerous out there.

But if there is, my stun-ray will knock it out. I'll have plenty of time to get away.

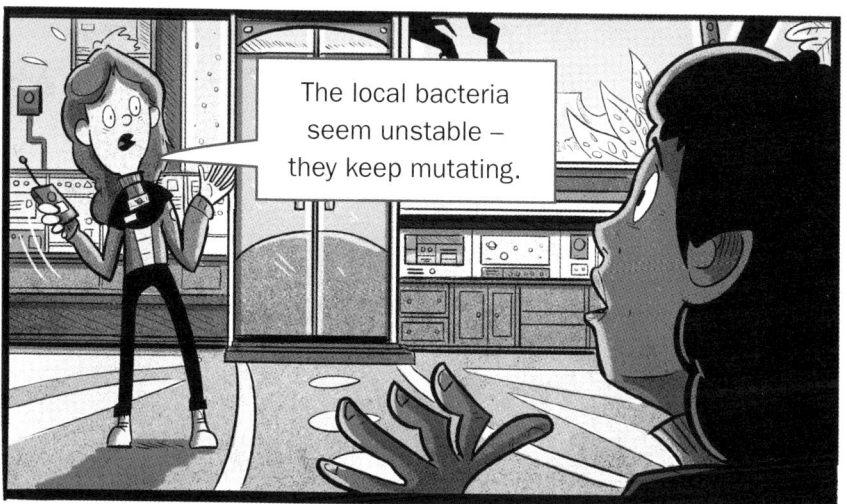

Captain, I've been out here for hours. This planet is clean.

Captain! One of our collectors brought this in a few minutes ago.
So what?

There's something creepy going on here ...

So, you want to play games, yeah?

Whatever's after me — I can't see them!

It's like that game we used to play when I was a kid …

What's the time, Mr Wolf?

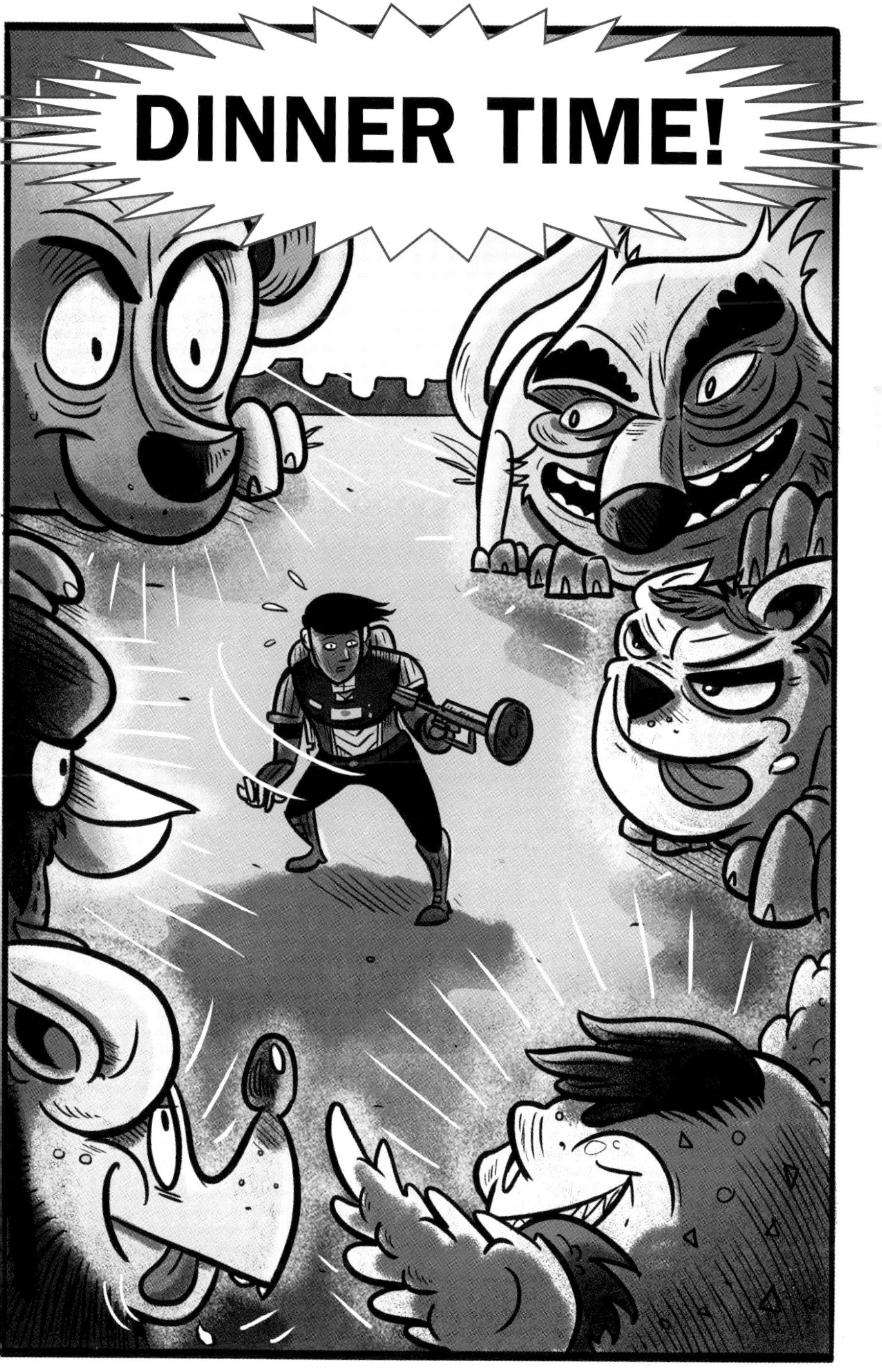
DINNER TIME!

A Trip to the Zoo

Written by Steve Barlow and Steve Skidmore
Illustrated by Mark Long

Setting the scene

HOLLY is a strong character in the group She is quite impatient.

EMMA is kind and caring.

TEZ is smart and confident. He often only does what he wants to do.

MUZZY is funny and is always joking around. Sometimes his jokes can seem a little mean.

JAROL: is a hologram.

The setting: The play is set in the present day. Holly, Emma, Tez and Muzzy are friends hanging out at Tez's house. They are starting to get bored.

Scene 1

Interior, present day. The living room in Tez's house. TEZ and MUZZY are sitting on a sofa. HOLLY is looking over their shoulders at the new tablet computer on which TEZ is playing a game. EMMA is staring into a glass tank containing a tropical habitat for reptiles.

TEZ: Yes! I've landed on the alien planet!

HOLLY: There's an alien! … No, it's a bush, sorry.

TEZ: I'm on it, Holly.

MUZZY: Look out! The alien's hiding behind the bush. *(Muzzy leans over.)*

HOLLY: Told you.

TEZ: *(pressing 'play' again)* It got me! 'Game over'. I'll have to start the level again.

HOLLY: Hey, Em! What are you doing?

EMMA: Watching Tez's lizard.

HOLLY joins EMMA and watches the lizard in the tank impatiently for a few moments.

HOLLY: *(rapping on the glass tank)* Why doesn't it move?

TEZ: Don't do that, Holly!

HOLLY: Well, your stupid newt won't do anything interesting.

TEZ: It's not a newt. It's a bearded dragon.

HOLLY: It's boring, Tez. Why do you keep it?

EMMA: They're just miserable. How'd you like to spend your life in a tank with people gawping at you?

MUZZY: Go on, Tez! You've got the alien on the run this time …

EMMA: You've been playing on that thing for hours.

TEZ: So? I only bought it yesterday.

MUZZY: It has leap motion, a nano plasma drive, DVI, ECC …

HOLLY: *(in a mocking voice) PTO, RSVP, LOL …*

EMMA: Whatever. Can't we go out?

The others stare at EMMA.

TEZ: Go out?

EMMA: Go outside. Get some fresh air, see places, meet people - you know, do *some*thing!

TEZ: We can do all that here. *(waving his tablet)* With this, we can go anywhere we like on the net.

EMMA: I want fresh air …

MUZZY: Put your head out of the window then! *(chuckles)*

45

EMMA: Come on, let's go somewhere – the park, the zoo …

MUZZY: Boring.

TEZ: No way. I'm gonna be surfing all day. *(tapping the screen)*

EMMA I want to go out.

HOLLY: Me too. I'm fed up of watching Tez play games and staring at his stupid newts …

TEZ: Lizards!

HOLLY: We definitely need a trip out. Tez, find something on the net. Search for 'out of this world day trip' or something.

TEZ: *(grudgingly)* OK. *(He taps the screen and reads.)* There's parachuting, go-kart racing, white-water rafting …

HOLLY: They cost a fortune. Isn't there anything free?

TEZ: You could try this.

EMMA: What is it?

MUZZY: A competition. *(He reads in a fake movie trailer voice.)* "Win the trip of a lifetime!"

HOLLY: Sounds good. You wanted to go on a trip, Em.

EMMA: I meant *today*. Not when they announce the winners in six months … anyway, we won't win it.

TEZ: Let's give it a go. *(He touches the screen and reads.)* Wow! First prize is a trip to an interplanetary zoo.

HOLLY: A zoo for aliens? I don't think so …

MUZZY: It's a wind up - it has to be.

TEZ: *(reads)* 'The lucky winners will meet strange alien beings.'

EMMA: *(turning to TEZ and MUZZY)* I already have … You two!

TEZ: Very funny, hah, hah! Let's find out more? It could be a laugh. *(reading aloud)* The question is: 'What is the name of your planet?'

MUZZY: *(rolling his eyes)* They always start with the hard ones first!

HOLLY: It's like the competitions they have on the telly. The questions are easy so everyone enters and the organizers get rich.

EMMA: It's just spam … It's not real.

TEZ: Then there's no harm in us entering, is there?

MUZZY: You wanted to visit faraway places Emma. Here's your chance.

TEZ: The answer is *(types)* 'Earth'.

There is a brief pause then music blasts out from the computer.

TEZ: *(shocked)* We've won!

HOLLY: *Already?* It's a wind up. It must be.

TEZ: *(reading aloud)* 'Our representative will be with you shortly!' I love the net – there's all kinds of crazy stuff on here.

EMMA: I don't like this, Tez … It feels wrong. Shut it down.

The room is filled with a blinding white light. When it fades, a holographic figure has appeared. It is dressed in a perfect uniform and its movements are human-like but oddly artificial. TEZ, MUZZY, HOLLY and EMMA stare at it open-mouthed.

HOLLY: Whoah! What is that?

JAROL: Greetings. I am Jarol.

TEZ: *(turns to JAROL)* How did you get in here?

JAROL: *(speaking in a robotic voice)* Do not be alarmed. I am not in the room with you in any physical sen … sen … sen … *(JAROL jerks his head awkwardly.)* sense.

MUZZY: Did you see that? He glitched! I get it – he's a hologram! Like in the movies.

Tez stares at his computer in awe.

TEZ: Projecting a hologram – Wow! I never knew my computer could do that!

JAROL: Congratulations! You have won our competition.

EMMA: I told you this was a bad idea.

JAROL: You have won the trip of a lifetime to our interplanetary zoo. You will come with me.

EMMA: We're not going anywhere!

TEZ: Of course we're not, Em. Stop worrying. *(turns to JAROL)* So if you're real and this zoo of yours is real, when do we go and how do we get there?

JAROL: Immediately – and like this …

A blinding white light fills the room. TEZ, HOLLY, EMMA and MUZZY scream. Fade to black.

Scene 2

Interior. They are in a white-walled room. They are dazed. One of the 'walls' is transparent – the characters behave as if there is an invisible barrier between themselves and the audience. The room has several Earth-style objects in it but they don't look quite like the real thing.

HOLLY: Where are we?

JAROL: You are in the zoo.

TEZ: This is weird.

EMMA: This can't be real.

MUZZY: *(trying to laugh off his unease)* You wanted an exciting day out, Emma. Looks like you've got it!

TEZ: No, but, seriously, where are we?

JAROL: This habitat was created especially for you. I hope you like it.

TEZ: *(pointing to a table with food on it)* Excellent! Snack time!

HOLLY: *(looking more closely at the food.)* Yeah, but …

JAROL: You must be hungry. Our observations indicate that your favourite foods is beefburgers and ice cream.

HOLLY: Yeah – but not together!

MUZZY: What?

TEZ: Look at this stuff! Baked beans on custard. Strawberries-and-cream with spaghetti …

JAROL: This is incorrect? I will have adjustments made. You must eat though. It is expected. It is part of the daily schedule.

MUZZY: Well, I'm starving. *(He picks up some of the food and begins to eat.)*

MUZZY: Blurgh!!! It tastes awful!

JAROL: Many apologies. Observing your planet was difficult. Our information for food replication must be incorrect. I have recorded this mistake. It is part of my role to observe you.

EMMA: *(worried)* Observe us?

JAROL: Yes. We want to learn more about your species over the coming days. I will now report back to our director.

JAROL stands completely still. EMMA and her friends look at each other. HOLLY waves a hand in front of JAROL's eyes. There is no reaction.

MUZZY: Maybe he's gone offline.

TEZ: Offline?

MUZZY: Well, he is a hologram.

HOLLY: What did he mean about observing us? We're the visitors here, right? I mean, when you go to the zoo, you watch the animals – they don't watch you …

EMMA: Gorillas do. Chimps and orangutans, too. I always wonder what they're thinking.

TEZ: *(swinging his arms and walking like a chimp)* Maybe it's time for another go on my tyre?

MUZZY: Trust Tez to get inside the mind of an ape!

EMMA: This is all just *odd*. I mean, we can't really be on an alien planet.

There is a thunderous knocking sound.
They jump and cower away from the noise.
MUZZY recovers first and points towards the transparent wall.

MUZZY: Whoah, look out there! There are aliens …

EMMA: They're all staring at us.

HOLLY: They are really strange-looking!

EMMA: Green heads. Purple bodies. Tentacles.

MUZZY: *(uncertainly)* They could be CGI*…

EMMA: Who'd spend millions on CGI aliens just to impress us?

MUZZY: But this can't be real. We can't be on some planet with a bunch of aliens. It's impossible, isn't it?

---

* Computer-generated image

EMMA: No, it isn't – this is real. We really are in an alien zoo …

HOLLY: *(pointing)* It's not like our zoos. We put different animals in different cages. These aliens are all jumbled together.

EMMA: *(sounds unsure)* Maybe the aliens aren't the animals.

TEZ: What do you mean?

HOLLY: That little one looks like it's carrying some kind of a doll.

MUZZY: It's not an alien doll, though – it's a human doll …

TEZ: It looks like you, Hol. It's wearing the same clothes … and its hair is done like yours …

HOLLY: *(horrified)* It is me!

MUZZY: And there's one that looks like me!

EMMA: From the souvenir shop.

HOLLY: What?

EMMA: When you go to the zoo, there's always a souvenir shop. They sell cuddly toys of the animals …

Jarol comes back to life.

JAROL: I have made my report. Your feeding requirements will be met.

HOLLY: *(worried)* Listen – it's been an amazing day but we've had enough.

EMMA: *(to HOLLY)* You still don't get it, do you? Think, how did we get here?

TEZ: The competition …

EMMA: How do you catch an animal? You offer it something it likes. It takes it then BANG! It's caught. Humans *love* competitions …

MUZZY: You're saying the competition was a trap? You mean …

EMMA: I mean Jarol isn't our guide – he's our zookeeper! We're not the visitors! *(pointing at the aliens beyond the 'wall')* They are! We're the animals!

JAROL: Indeed. You are our top attraction. All these visitors are here to see you.

TEZ: What?

JAROL: You wanted the trip of a lifetime. You have it. You will be here for the rest of your lives.

HOLLY: No … we can't … oh, no …

TEZ, MUZZY, HOLLY and EMMA turn to stare through the 'wall'. Thunderous knocking resumes.

TEZ: They're knocking on our tank.

HOLLY: *(screams)* Stop it! We're not stupid lizards!

MUZZY: They want us to move about more.

EMMA: They want us to do something interesting …

Fade to black.

Aliens!

I am a geek, a sci-fi freak,
I'm lost among the stars
With Doctor Who and Captain Kirk
And Little men from Mars…

For Cybermen and Daleks
Rampage across my dreams…
Wookies, Hutts and Ewoks, too
I wonder what it means?

I may have overdone it,
And now I'm in despair;
For night and day, all I can see
Are aliens everywhere!

Aliens, aliens in my head.
Aliens, aliens in my bed.
Aliens, aliens, in my shoe,
Aliens, aliens, down the loo.

Aliens, aliens, under floors,
Aliens, aliens, in my drawers.
Aliens, aliens in my hair!
Aliens, aliens everywhere!

I'm terrified of shadows, now.
I'm frightened of the dark.
Of flying saucers overhead,
And statues in the park (DON'T BLINK!)

I'm scared of little silver men,
ET gives me the jitters.
I'm not a chicken or a wimp,
Or one of nature's quitters –

But now I just can't stand it!
I'm going mad, I swear!
For in my dreams (here come the screams!)
Are aliens – everywhere!

Green and purple, pink and puce
Dribbling slimy alien juice.
Waving feelers, clicking claws.
Gnashing nasty alien jaws …

Here they come, from who-knows-where!
Hear that footstep on the stair?
What's that shadow by the chair?
Don't despair … you must prepare …
Close your eyes now, if you dare –
You'll see aliens everywhere!

Find out more ...

Join Team X on an adventure in space in *Theft in Space*

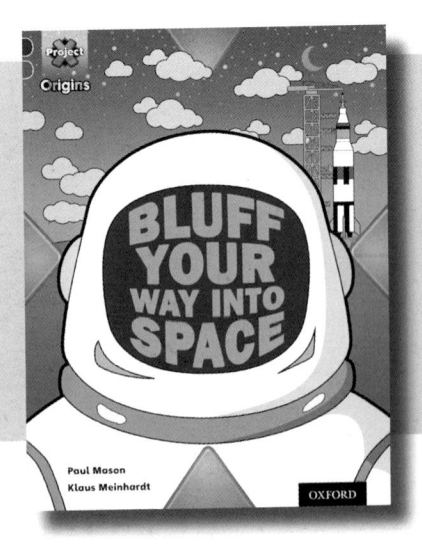

Ever wanted to go into space? Read *How to Bluff your way into space*